DRAGONS

Maarten Hesselt van Dinter

DRAGONS

Chinese-Japanese-Medieval Dragons

MUNDURUCU

PUBLISHERS

Research & concept: Maarten Hesselt van Dinter

Editor: Mark Poysden

Please use these images freely for your own requirements and as a source of inspiration. However, for commercial, promotional or professional use please contact the publisher for permission and fees: info@mundurucu.com.

ISBN: 978-90-78900-03-0

Visit the video and photo galleries at www.mundurucu.com for more dragons, fabulous creatures and tribal designs.

WWW.MUNDURUCU.COM

CONTENTS

Dragons

Dragons are winged creatures portrayed in the ancient mythologies of most cultures. They are linked to winged gods who came to Earth from the heavens to create the human race. Their universality is remarkable and a common origin is suggested by the many similarities in depictions of dragons across the globe. The dragon features in many legendary battles between the powers of darkness and light and good and evil.

In the West, dragons were considered loathsome beasts with malicious designs on humankind. As the myth developed in the West, dragons came to represent the chaos before matter took form. Many now believe that dragons and other serpentine creatures represented the earth and that all confrontations with such creatures are metaphors for man's battle to dominate the earth.

One of the earliest records of a dragon occurs in the legendary battle of the Babylonian god Marduk, also known as Bel, and the dragon Tiamat. Tiamat is described as a ferocious, scaly monster with wings and terrifying claws, sometimes with the body of a huge serpent, and sometimes with an animal's body (pp. 9, 40). In Greek mythology Cadmus, a Phoenician prince, battles with a guardian water-dragon after it killed some of his companions (pp. 31, 51, 52, 78, 79).

The Latin name for dragons, *draco*, is derived from the Greek name *drakon*, which means 'giant snake'. Indeed, in many tales the dragon is depicted or described as a large snake with ferocious teeth and a large tail. In Greek mythology, for example, Apollo, the son of Zeus, kills the monstrous winged beast (or dragon) called Python that protected the sanctuary of Delphi (pp. 27, 30). The dragon killed by Siegfried in *The Ring of the Nibelung* is often depicted as a snake (p. 82), as is the dragon that appears in legends in the *Arabian Nights* and the Persian *Book of Kings*, the *Shahnameh* (pp. 83, 26).

Dragons are usually depicted as huge multi-headed beasts. Hercules slew the Lernaean Hydra, a horrendous serpent with nine grotesque heads. Hydra was the offspring of the hundred-headed Typhon, an enormous giant with snake coils instead of legs. For each head Hercules cut off two new ones grew in its place. Aided by his nephew Iolaos, he eventually kills the monster with burning trees, which he used to scorch Hydra's heads one by one (pp. 10, 11).

A dragon is also described in the Bible. It is a multi-headed monster identified with the Antichrist or Satan. In the Book of Revelation an enormous beast rises from the sea, with seven heads and ten horns, 'each with a crown and all marked with the name of blasphemy' (p. 94, 95). The archangel Michael battles Satan in the form of a dragon and casts him out (p. 44). Another dragon-like monster that appears in the bible is Leviathan, a large sea-monster. In the Old Testament, the Book of Job 3.8 states: 'May those who curse days curse that day, those who are ready to rouse Leviathan' (pp. 133).

A similar monster appears in Greek mythology: When Perseus returned home after killing Medusa, one of the Gorgons, the sight of whom turned people to stone, he encountered the beautiful Andromeda chained to a rock. In order to appease Poseidon, her father King Cepheus decided to sacrifice her to the terrible sea-snake Ceto, but Perseus slew the monster and claimed Andromeda as his wife (p. 48, 49).

Probably the most famous battle between a man and a dragon, the originally Eastern legend of St George and the Dragon bears many similarities to the Perseus and Andromeda myth (and even may have served as its inspiration). The earliest known surviving narrative is an 11th-century Georgian text. The myth was brought back to Europe with returning Crusaders. A dragon tormenting a small town in Libya is first appeased with sheep, before the desperate villagers feed it their children. When the lot falls on the king's daughter, St George comes to her rescue, but he only killed the dragon after the king and his subjects converted to Christianity. In Christianity dragons symbolised sin and old animist beliefs, and saints such as St George were shown triumphing over them (p. 18, 19, 32, 33, 45).

Medieval texts describe dragons as warm-blooded, winged creatures that live in caves in India and Ethiopia. They have large claws and their bodies are completely covered with tough, shiny scales (pp. 84, 100, 101). They cause harm by lashing out with their tails, with which they catch (preferably) elephants (p. 97). Such dragon stories often originated from encounters with unknown animals in newly discovered territories (pp. 108, 109).
In comparison to Ethiopian dragons, European dragons often breathed fire (p. 85, 131). They lived in caves, mountains or lakes, guarding treasures and, because they preyed upon the weak, were often challenged by knights.

In the Middle Ages, dragons were used as warlike emblems in many European cultures – carved on the prows of Norse ships, for example – and various European families adopted dragons as their ensigns. Heraldic crests, body armour and shields often depicted dragons or dragon-like creatures. Knights wanted to be associated with the attributes of these creatures: besides its malevolence the Western dragon was known for its keen sight, power, and fearsomeness. The wyvern, a dragon-like creature with only two legs, was believed to symbolise power and strength, important features in battle (pp. 130, 143, 144). The cockatrice, produced from a cock's egg hatched by a serpent, and the basilisk with its rooster-shaped head and draconic-body, were both known for their deadly stare and their venom (pp. 140, 141, 146).

Dragons have an important role in the alchemical world and symbolised several principles of nature. A dragon shrouded in flames for example, represented fire and calcination (p. 115); several dragons fighting symbolised putrefaction (p. 117); dragons with wings represented the volatile principle (p. 114) and dragons without wings the fixed principle. Ouroboros, a dragon swallowing its own tail and forming a circle was the most widely used. It symbolised the cyclical nature of alchemy (pp. 105, 118, 119).

9

Marduk (Bel) and the dragon
Babylonian mythology

The terrifying Hydra

Hercules battling Hydra

Mechanical dragon
15th century

Mechanical practise dragon
15th century

14

Illuminated letter
12th century

Illuminated letter
15th century

Medieval dragon

Persian dragon
16th century

Illuminated letter depicting St George and the dragon
Italy, 1340

Illuminated letter depicting St George and the dragon
15th century

The Whore of Babylon
Book of Revelation, Chapter 17

The virgin St Margaret and the dragon

Dragon from East India

French medieval dragon
c. 1570

Moses performs magic at the Egyptian court
Exodus 7.9-12

St Margaret and the dragon
17th century

Persian dragon from the *Shahnameh*
c. 1100

The dragon killed by Apollo
16th-century depiction

The Apocalypse
Book of Revelation 13.1

Dragon from the Apocalypse

Apollo and the dragon
15th-century depiction

Cadmus and the dragon
15th-century depiction

St George and the dragon
Albrecht Dürer, 16th century

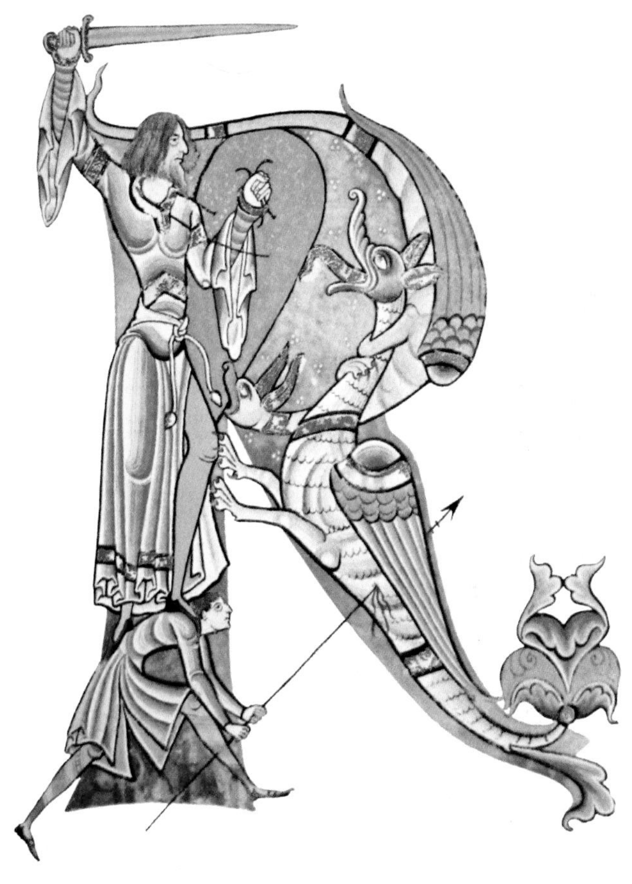

Illuminated letter depicting St George and the dragon
12th century

Illuminated letter
Saxon, 9th century

Illuminated letter
Saxon, 9th century

36

Persian dragon
16th century

Illuminated letter from the Bible
12th century

Illuminated letter
12th century

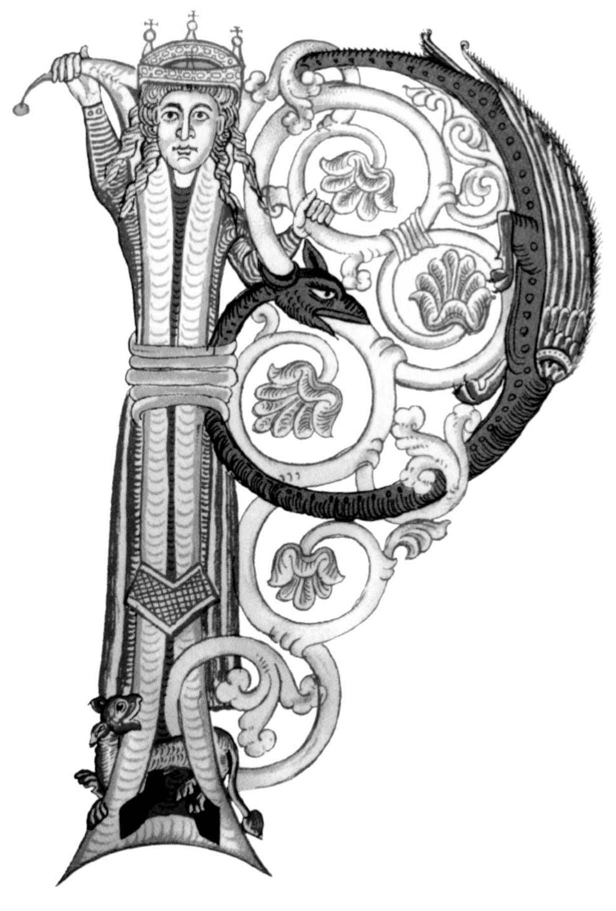

Illuminated letter
12th century

Dragon of Marduk (Tiamat)
c. 600 BC

Persian dragon
16th century

42

Illuminated letter
German, 13th century

Ornamental dragons
15th century

St Michael and the dragon
c. 1260

St George and the dragon
Paolo Uccello, c. 1460

Perseus saves Andromeda
Greek mythology

Perseus saves Andromeda
16th-century depiction

50

Dragon chariot of Demeter
Greek mythology

Cadmus, the Dragon Slayer
Phoenician mythology

The dragon devouring the companions of Cadmus
16th-century depiction

Jason sedates the dragon
16th-century depiction

Dragon chariot of Ceres
Greek mythology

Ship of the Argonauts
16th-century depiction

Trojan dragon

Apocalyptic dragon

58

The Dragon from Rhodos
Part 1

59

The Dragon from Rhodos
Part 2

The Dragon from Rhodos
Part 3

The Dragon from Rhodos
Part 4

62

French dragon
14th century

French dragon
14th century

French dragons
14th century

French dragon
14th century

French dragon
14th century

Dragon with young
17th century

Winged dragon
19th century

Winged dragon
19th century

Celtic dragon

Celtic dragon

Medieval Celtic dragon
6th century

Celtic dragon
9th century

Celtic dragon
11th century

Classical Roman dragon

Celtic dragons

Bermuda dragon

Cadmus and the dragon
15th-century depiction

Cadmus killing the dragon
15th-century depiction

The Dragon from Rhodos
c. 1350

Two-footed winged dragon
16th century

Dragon from *The Rhinegold & the Valkyrie*
Arthur Rackham, 1912

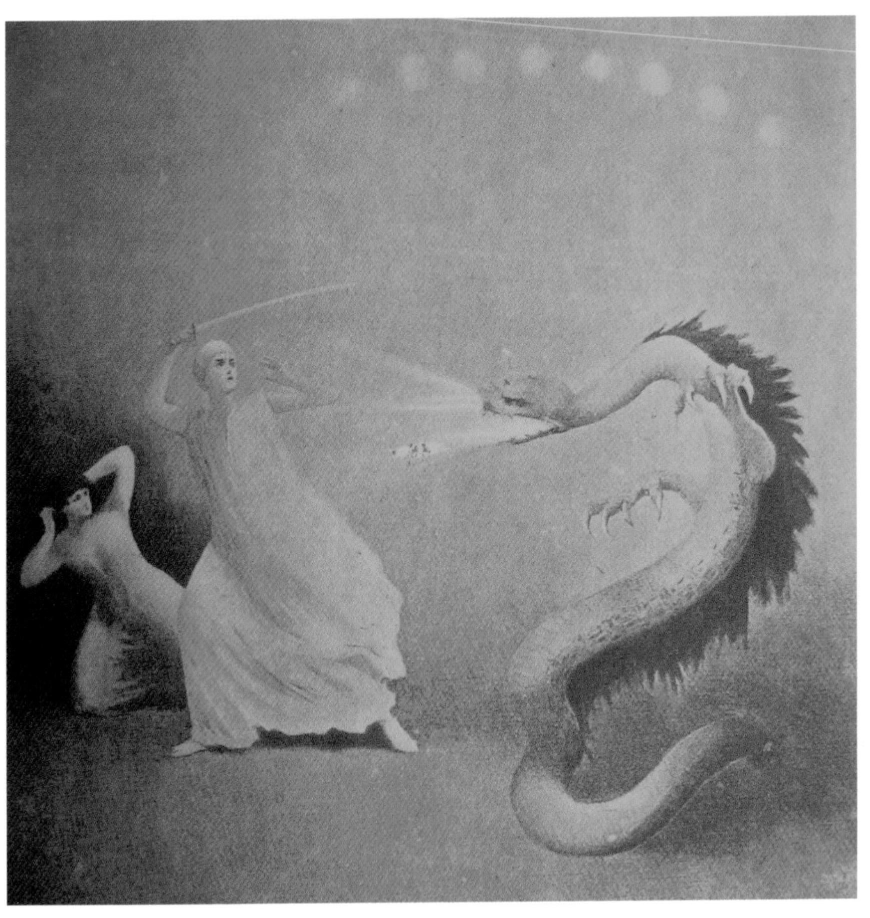

Dragon from *The Arabian Nights*

Ethiopian winged dragon
16th century

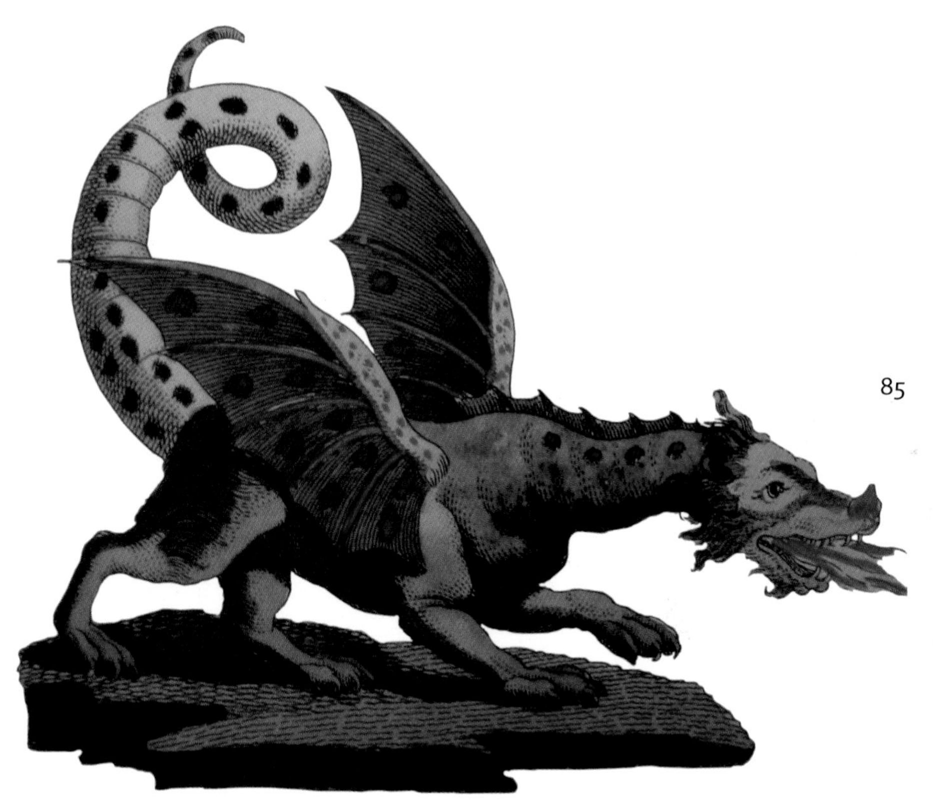

Medieval dragon
18th-century depiction

Hydra septiceps
16th century

Hydra septiceps
16th century

Winged dragon
Aldrovandi, 16th century

Winged dragon
Aldrovandi, 16th century

90

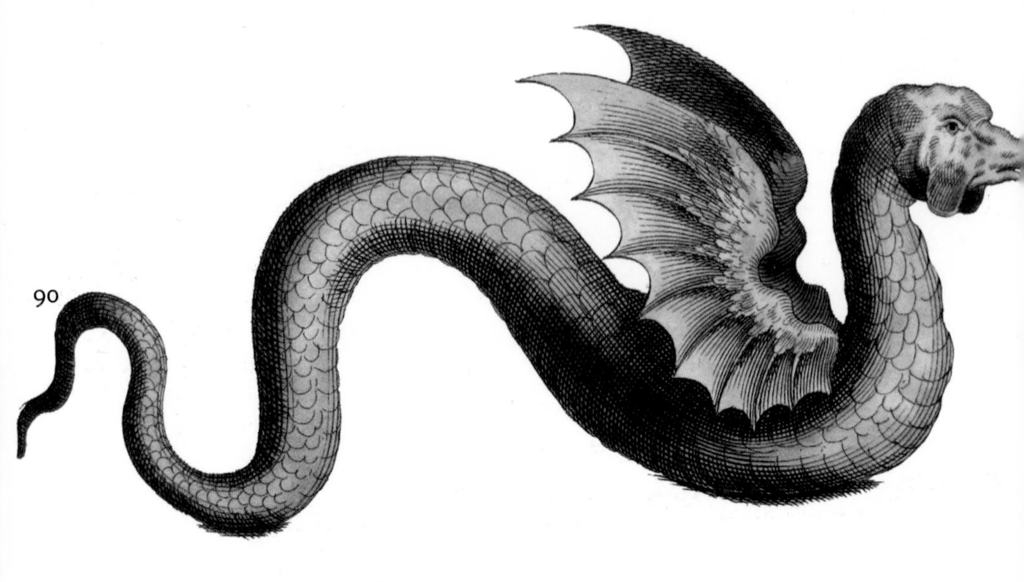

Dog-faced winged dragon
Aldrovandi, 16th century

Two-footed wingless dragon
Aldrovandi, 16th century

Apocalyptic dragon
France, c. 1100

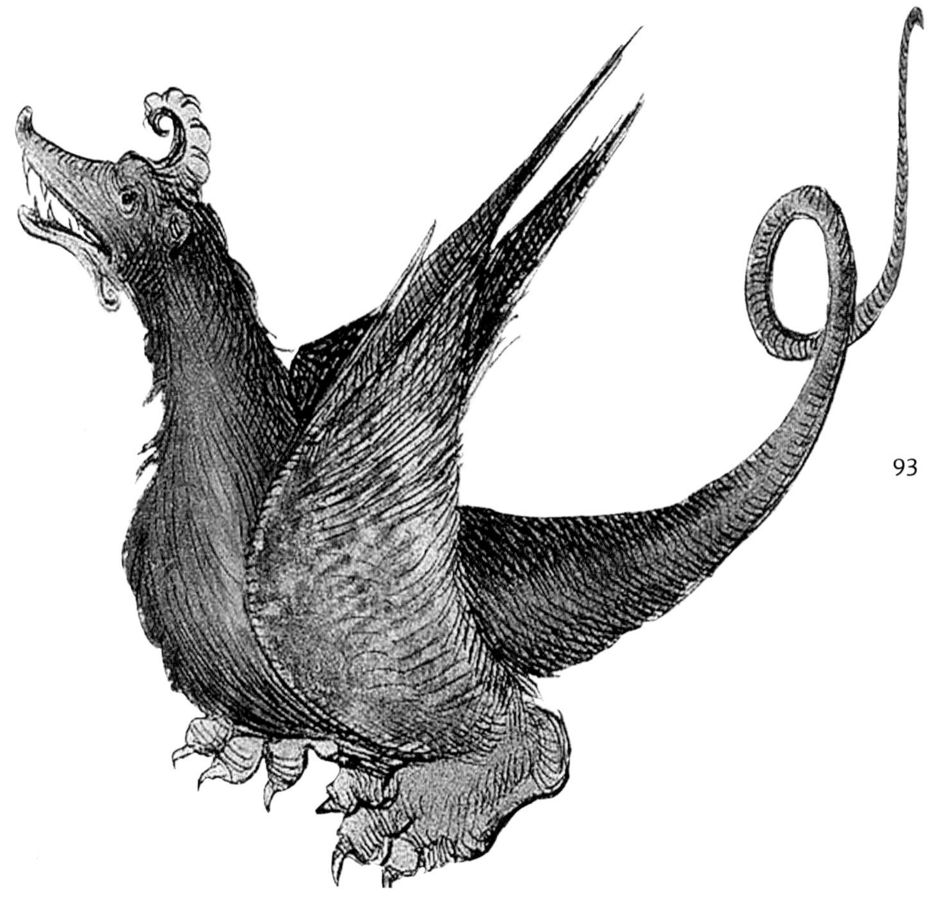

Flemish dragon
c. 1460

The Red Dragon
c. 1250

Dragon from the Apocalypse
Book of Revelation 12.3-4

King Basilisk
16th century

Elephant-strangling dragon

Elephant-killing dragon
16th century

Elephant-killing dragon
16th century

100

Dragon from Georgia
16th century

Two-legged winged dragon
1640

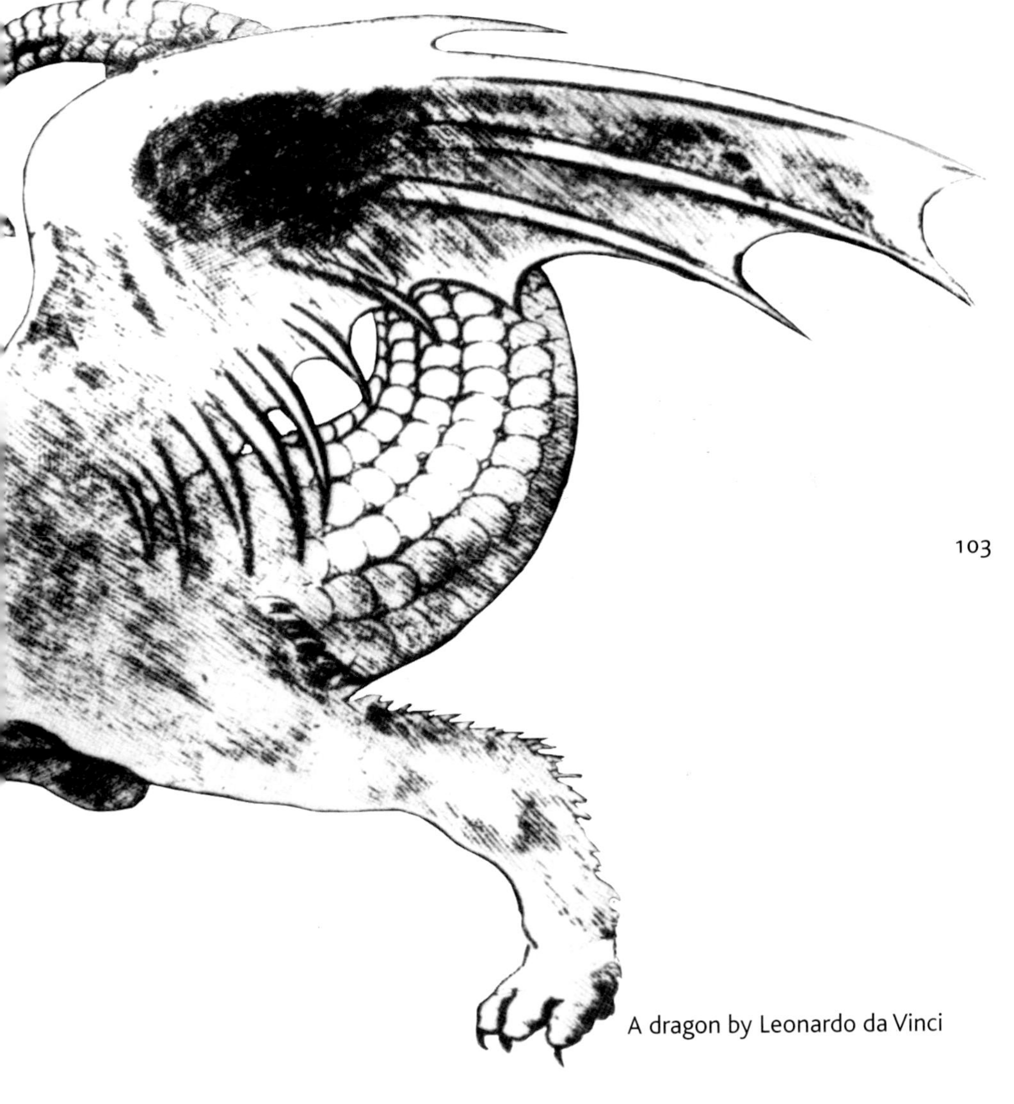

A dragon by Leonardo da Vinci

Little French dragon
15th century

Ouroboros

Sea dragons in the Erythraean Sea
16th century

Sea dragon in a Roman arena
16th-century depiction

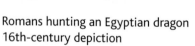

Romans hunting an Egyptian dragon
16th-century depiction

Romans killing an Egyptian dragon
16th-century depiction

Dragon slaying in India
16th century

Dragon slaying in Egypt
16th century

Alchemical dragon
17th century

Killing an alchemical dragon

Alchemical dragon symbolising the volatile principle
1624

Alchemical dragon symbolising fire
1570

116

The Crucified Snake
14th century

Alchemical dragons symbolising putrefaction
14th century

Ouroboros

Ouroboros

Dragon of Wantley
19th-century depiction

Mantygre (Man-Tiger)

Dragon of St Germain
15th century

Dragon of Wantley
17th-century depiction

Cambodian dragon

Dragon from Barcelona

Turkish dragon
17th century

Dragon from Georgia
18th century

English dragon
1641

The Husband-Eating Bigorne
French folklore

130

English wyvern

Dragon of Wantley
18th-century depiction

Man in Hell
c. 1650

Destruction of Leviathan
Gustave Doré, 1860

Sea monster sighted in 1834

Sea monster sighted at Helgeland in 1560

Sea monster sighted in 1640

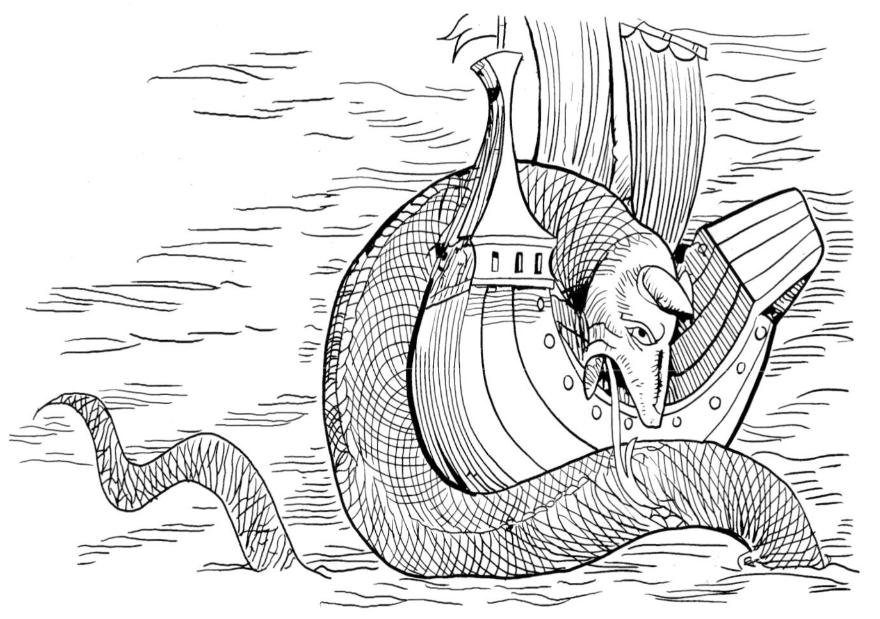

Sea monster sighted in 1580

Heraldic wyvern

Arms of the City of London
c. 1900

Heraldic cockatrice

Heraldic basilisk

Ornamental dragon
1284

Heraldic wyvern
1436

Heraldic wyvern

Heraldic dragon

Heraldic cockatrice

Dragon of Cadwallader

148

A dragon crest

A wyvern crest

Chained dragon's head

Supporter of arms

Calligraphic dragon
England, 17th century

Calligraphic dragon
England, 17th century

154

Calligraphic dragon
England, 17th century

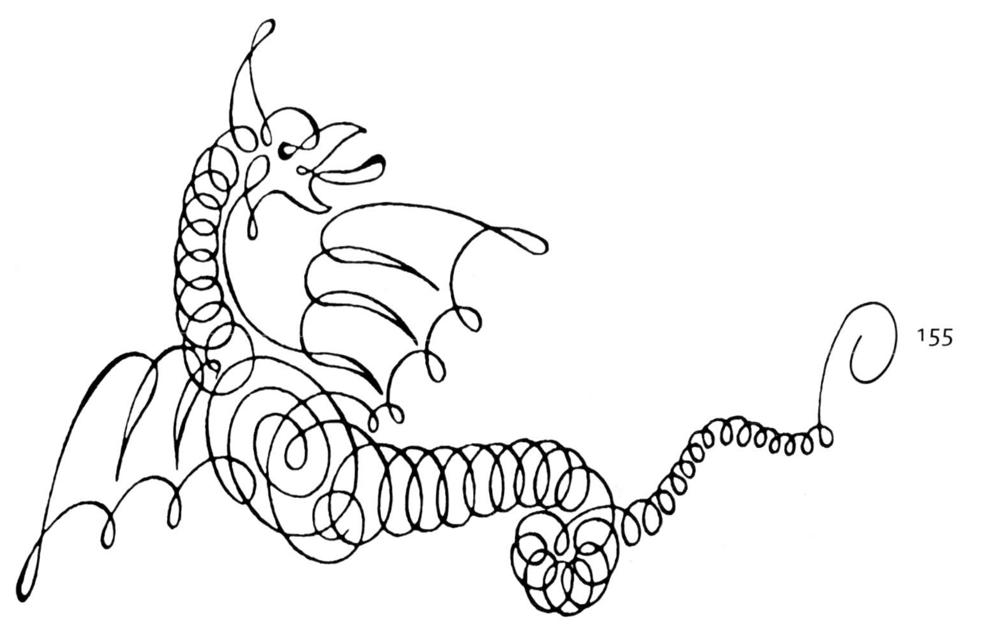

Calligraphic dragon
England, 17th century

Oriental dragons

'The Dragon with the formidable flash of his eyes, the fierce strike of his claws, the brooding silence of his slumber in deep waters, and his triumphant soaring above the black of thunder-clouds fitly symbolised the demoniac quality that entered into the nature of the Pontiff Emperor's sovereignty. At one time remote, ascetic, divested of every early thought and passion to become a pure vessel for receiving divine blessings and transmitting them to the people, at another the terrifying executioner of the justice and wrath of God.' (A. E. Grantham, *Hills of Blue*, 1927).

In contrast to the Western perception of dragons, in the Far East dragons are rarely malevolent. Though they may be fearsome and are extremely powerful, they are primarily considered just, benevolent, and the bringers of wealth and good fortune. The appearance of dragons in early Eastern and Western astronomy is due to them supposedly being the enemies of the sun and the moon. Eclipses occur when a dragon attempts to swallow either of these heavenly bodies.

Dragons are thought to be aquatic, living at the bottom of the sea, where they guard vast treasure hoards, usually pearls. They also live in and control rivers, lakes and rain, and the larger the expanse of water, the more powerful the dragon. Sea dragons generally have no wings. In ancient legends, the Dragon God caused the phosphorescence that occasionally illumines the sea. Dragon shrines and altars can still be seen in many parts of the Far East, usually along seashores and riverbanks. Despite their wisdom, Oriental dragons were vain and quickly affronted if ignored by the rulers they advised, or if they were not honoured. They could stop producing rain by thrashing about, or exhale black clouds that brought storms and floods.

According to a description from 1100 BC, Chinese dragons had the head of a camel, the horns of a deer, the eyes of a hare, the ears of a bull, the scales of a carp, the paws of a tiger, claws resembling those of an eagle, and whiskers. Moreover, dragons are deaf, can expand or contract their bodies, and can transform themselves or become invisible.

The Chinese Dragon, *lung* (or *long*), symbolises power and excellence, boldness, heroism and perseverance, nobility and divinity. In the Far East, dragons overcome obstacles until achieving success. They are energetic, decisive, optimistic, intelligent and ambitious. In China dragons, wind and life are one, and they dominate the clouds and the rains of heaven. Clouds owe their divine character to dragons, but they are also dependent on them. Chinese dragons are therefore often depicted among clouds.

The emperors of China adopted the dragon as their symbol, an emblem of supreme power and immortality. Starting with the Yuan Dynasty (1271–1368), ordinary citizens were forbidden from associating themselves with the symbol. The first Ming emperor even introduced strict edicts regulating the design of the dragon and decreed that the five-clawed dragon be used on his robes to indicate his superiority. The number of claws the Chinese dragon had was also officially prescribed: dragons with five claws on each of the four paws were reserved for the Emperor, four for the nobles and three for the commoners. Similar rules applied to the Imperial dragon-boat. The emperor's throne, banners and hangings were also decorated with dragon symbols.

A particular attribute of Oriental dragons is a magic pearl or ball, sometimes enveloped in flames. Depictions of dragons frequently show them chasing this jewel among clouds. This jewel is said to be the repository of great magic power, which the dragon tries to add to his trove of treasures. It has the power to multiply whatever it touches, symbolises spiritual perfection and wisdom and is a powerful good luck charm.

Dragons were also revered beyond the central empire. Texts written in the Lolo language of the aboriginal tribes of China indicate that these tribes had the same respect for dragons as in the rest of China (pp. 184, 185).

Chinese literature refers to many types and names of dragons. Around 300 BC, dragons were believed to preside over the seasons. The Green Dragon or spirit dragon was identified with the spring and the east; the White Dragon with autumn and the west; the Black Dragon ruled the north and was associated with winter and the Red and Yellow Dragon ruled the summer and south.
Chinese mythology records other types of dragons as well. For example earth dragons, masters of rivers and seas; celestial dragons, guardians of the dwellings of the gods; the coiling dragon, which lives in water; the hidden treasure dragon; the fish-dragon (p. 245); winged dragons that ride on clouds and mist, and Dragon Kings, each of which rules over one of the four seas to the east, south, west, and north.

The Japanese dragon, *ryu*, can generally be distinguished from other East-Asian dragons in that it has only three toes, rather than the *long's* five or the *ryong's* four. The *ryu* has its origins in China and is one of the four divine beasts of Japanese mythology. The other three are the crimson bird (phoenix), the black turtle and the white tiger. The *ryu* is frequently the emblem of the Emperor or a hero.

Ornamental armillary sphere
16th century

Chinese dragon
18th century

Chinese dragon
18th century

Chinese dragon
18th century

164

Chinese dragon
18th century

Chinese dragon
18th century

166

Chinese dragon
18th century

Chinese dragon
18th century

Chinese dragon
18th century

Chinese dragon
18th century

Chinese dragon

Chinese dragon
18th century

Chinese Imperial banner

Xiaosheng Empress Dowager
1751

174

Chinese dragon
19th century

Chinese dragon
19th century

Chinese dragon

Pendant with mirrored dragons

大鍾

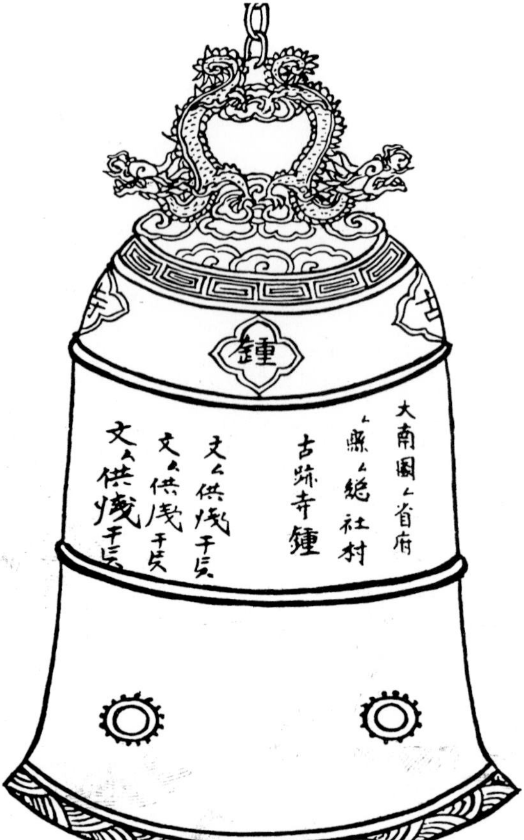

Ceremonial bell

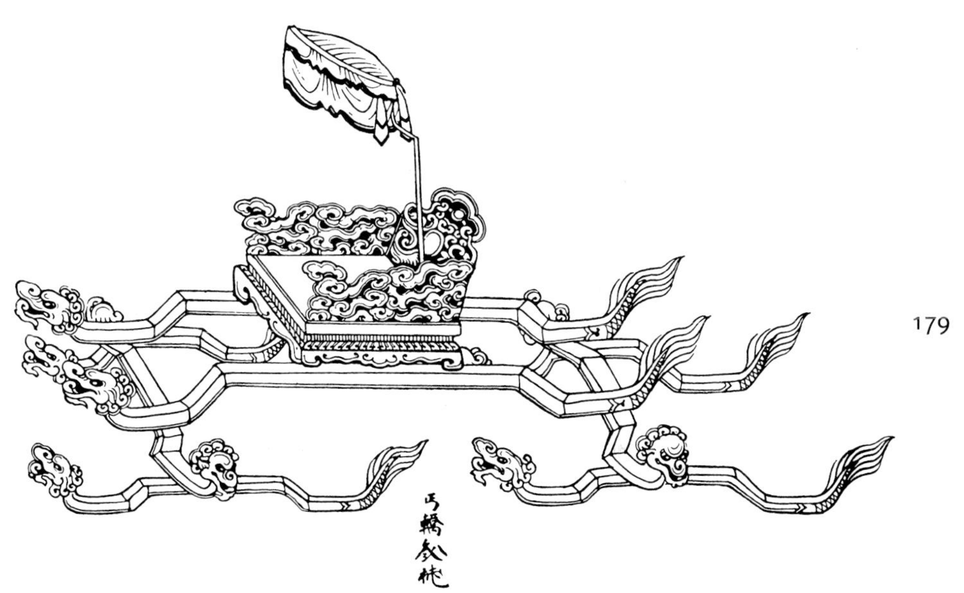

Ceremonial sedan chair

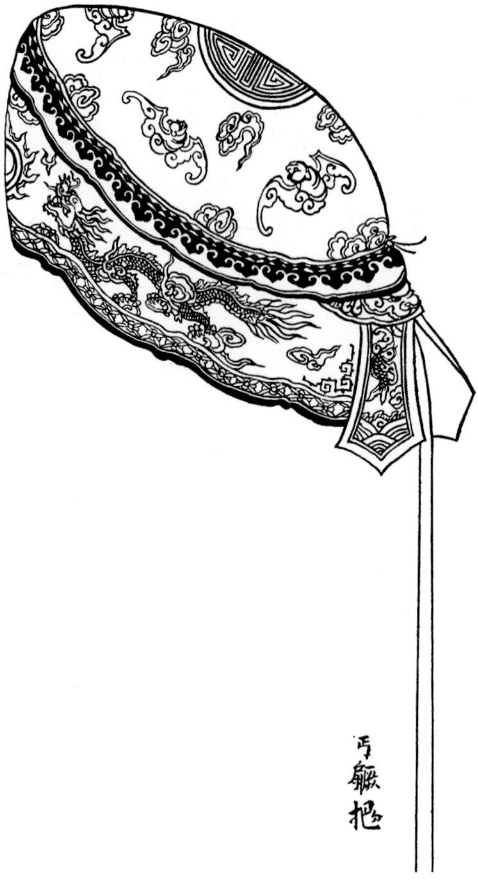

Embroidered parasol

Embroidered parasol

182

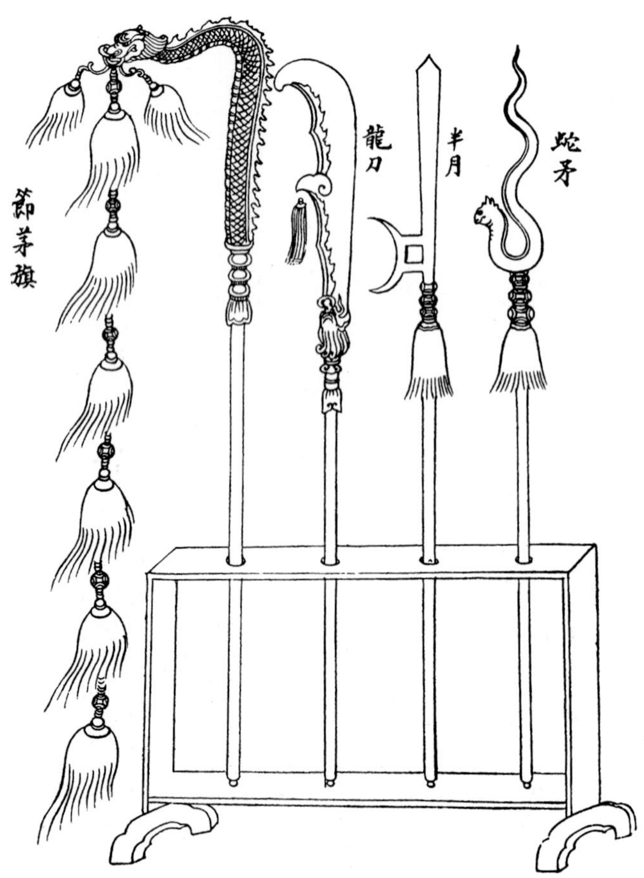

Ceremonial weapons

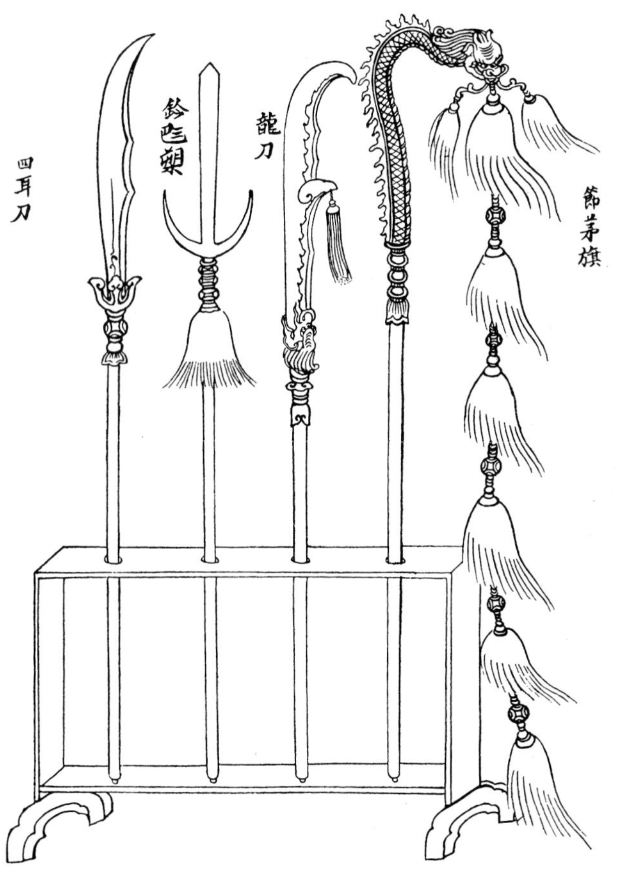

183

Ceremonial weapons

Lolo dragon

185

Lolo dragon

The Four Celestial Guardians

Dragon
Qingling period, c 1600

The Typhoon Dragon

Thunder Dragon

192

The Emperor K'i
Hai Dynasty (2200 BC)

The Spirit of the Yellow River
Hai Dynasty (2200 BC)

194

Chinese dragon design

Chinese dragon
17th century

Emperor Kangxi (1654–1722)

Emperor Kangxi, aged 32

Emperor Qianlong (1711–99)

Chinese emperor
17th century

Dragon amidst clouds

Dragons amidst clouds

202

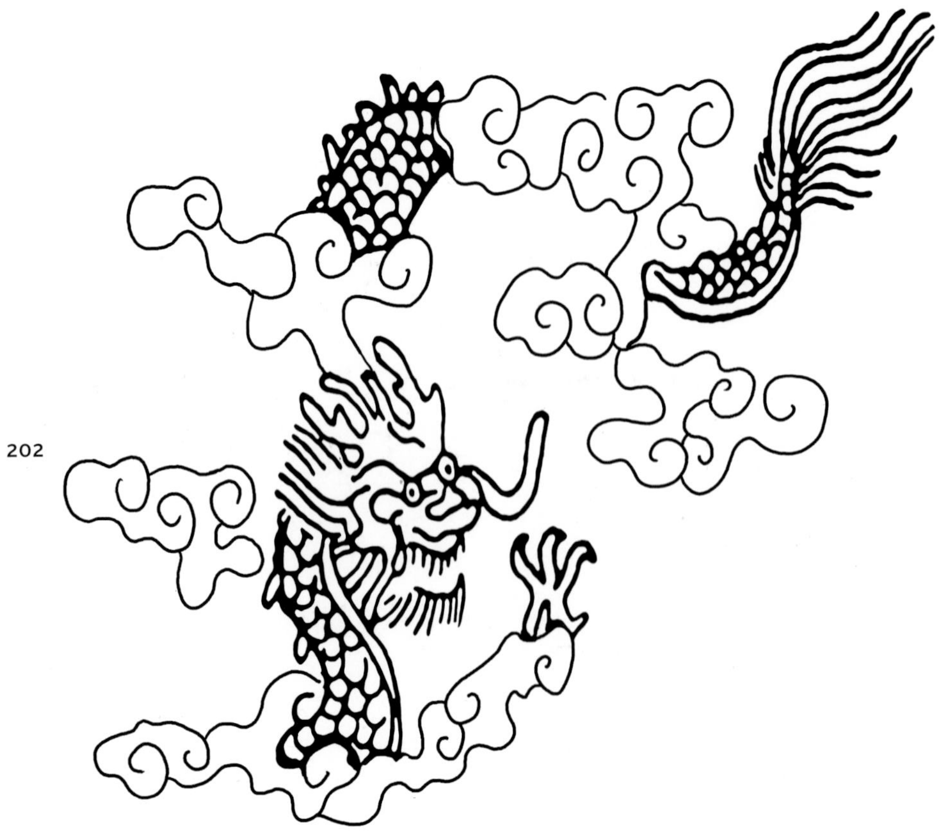

Dragon amidst clouds

Dragon amidst clouds

204

Mandarin ship
16th century

205

Chinese dragon boat

Imperial dragon boat

Imperial dragon boat

208

Boat for the Imperial concubines

209

Imperial dragon boat
c. 1660

The Eight Immortals crossing the sea

Tsing-Chen, Spirit of the Wells

The Imperial Dragon Throne
c. 1665

The Viceroy of China
1665

216

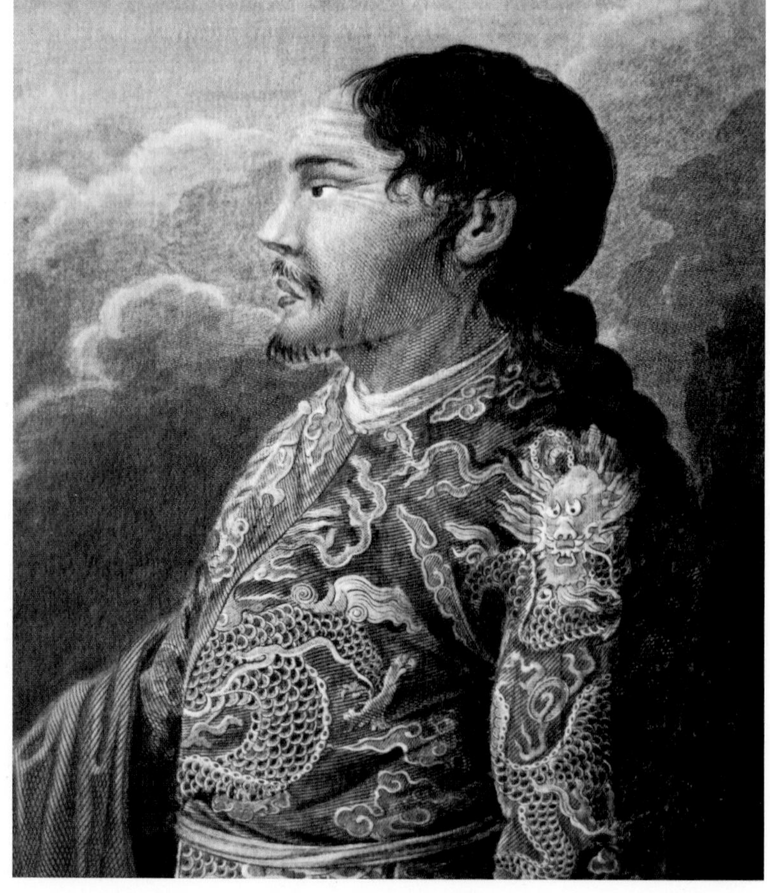

Imperial ceremonial dress
c. 1650

Chinese officials
c. 1650

218

Emperor Qianlong
1758

Japanese dragon
Utagawa Kuniyoshi (1798–1861)

220

Japanese dragon
Hokusai (1760–1849)

Japanese sea-dragon
Utagawa Kuniyoshi (1798–1861)

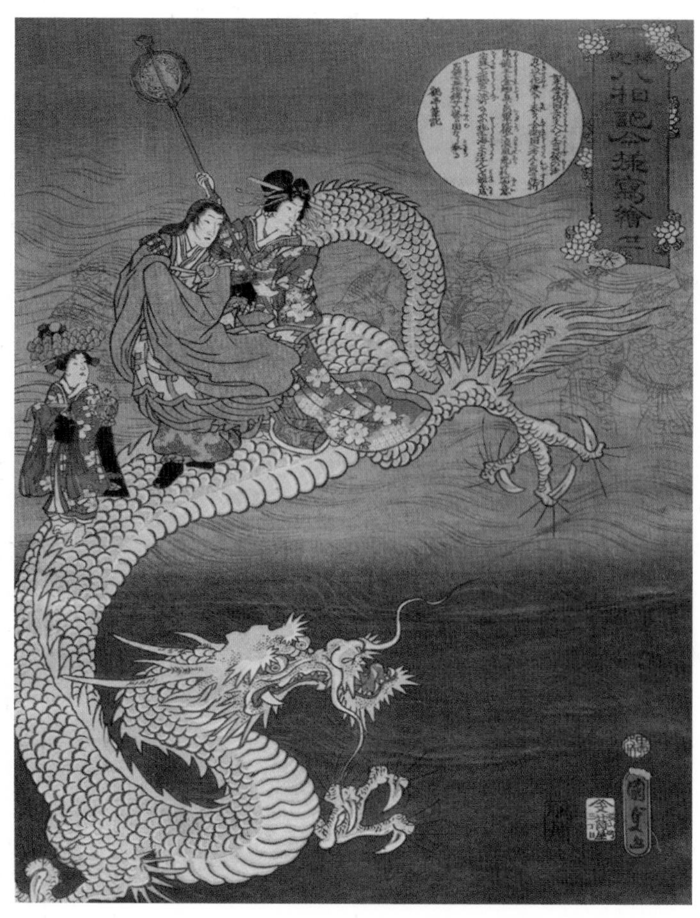

White Dragon
Utagawa Kunisada, c. 1860

Japanese dragon

Japanese dragon boat
c. 1660

The Red Dragon Boat

Dragon confronting a tiger
17th century

Dispute between a dragon and a tiger

Chinese dragon

龍

Imperial dragon

Decorative double dragon

Thunder dragons

两竜朝月

Dragons fighting over the moon

樞廷東閣

Chinese Dragons
Sung Dynasty (960–1279)

The Dragon Horse

Dragon with good luck symbol

Chinese dragon
11th century

Buddhist dragon

Chinese dragon
11th century

Chinese dragon-monster
11th century

Dragon
Ming Dynasty (1368–1644)

Imperial dragon from Manchus

242

Imperial dragon

Dragon
Northern Song Dynasty (960–1127)

244

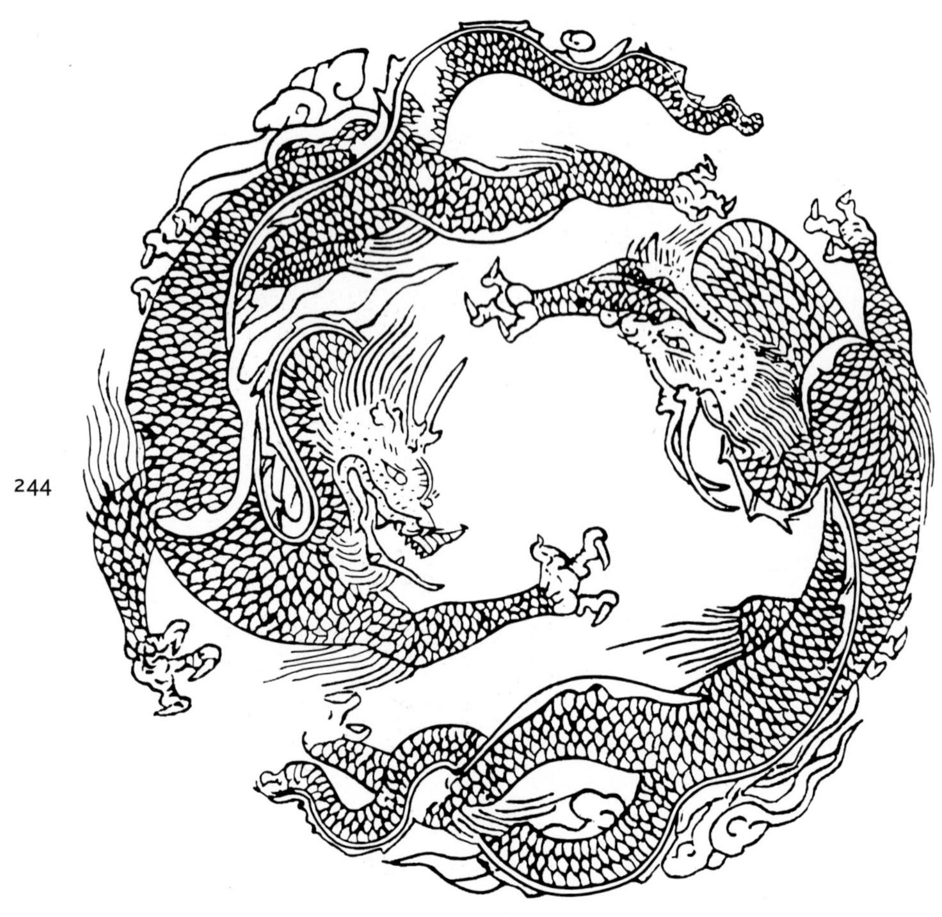

Dragons
Liao Dynasty (916–1125)

245

Makara, the Fish Dragon
10th-century depiction

The Flying Dragon

Classical *long* dragon
Ming Dynasty (1368–1644)

Japanese dragon

Japanese dragon

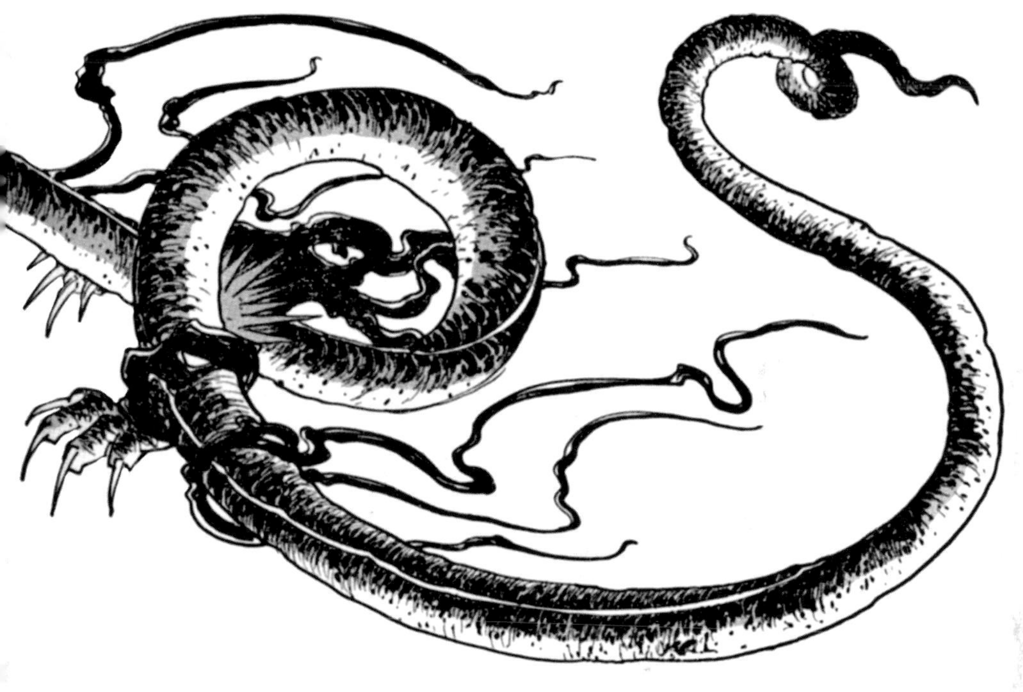

Multi-headed Japanese dragon

Japanese dragon
18th century

Japanese dragon
18th century

Japanese dragon

Japanese dragon

256

Bird dragon (*Hai ryu*)